50 Slow-Cooked Italian Comfort Foods

By: Kelly Johnson

Table of Contents

- Classic Italian Beef Ragu
- Osso Buco alla Milanese
- Slow-Cooked Lasagna
- Italian Braised Short Ribs
- Chicken Cacciatore
- Polenta with Slow-Cooked Mushrooms
- Tuscan Bean and Sausage Stew
- Italian Meatballs in Tomato Sauce
- Slow-Cooked Porchetta
- Vitello Tonato (Veal with Tuna Sauce)
- Risotto alla Milanese
- Slow-Cooked Bolognese Sauce
- Stracciatella Soup (Italian Egg Drop Soup)
- Slow-Cooked Eggplant Parmesan
- Osso Buco with Risotto
- Zuppa Toscana (Tuscan Soup)
- Slow-Cooked Italian Sausage and Peppers
- Gnocchi with Slow-Cooked Pork Ragu
- Slow-Cooked Veal Piccata
- Beef Braciole
- Pasta Fagioli
- Slow-Cooked Lamb Shanks with Garlic and Rosemary
- Slow-Cooked Pollo alla Romana
- Slow-Braised Capon
- Italian-Inspired Slow-Cooked Pork Roast
- Stewed Chickpeas with Garlic and Herbs
- Slow-Cooked Risotto with Mushrooms
- Slow-Cooked Risotto alla Milanese with Saffron
- Frittata di Patate (Potato Frittata)
- Pasta alla Norma (Eggplant and Ricotta)
- Minestrone Soup
- Slow-Cooked Goulash with Italian Sausage
- Italian-American Chicken Parmigiana
- Slow-Cooked Ziti with Sausage and Cheese
- Ribollita (Tuscan Bread Soup)

- Slow-Cooked Tomato and Basil Soup
- Slow-Cooked Pappardelle with Wild Boar Ragu
- Pork Saltimbocca
- Slow-Cooked Sicilian Meatloaf
- Braised Fennel with Parmesan
- Italian Style Braised Brussels Sprouts
- Slow-Cooked Beef and Red Wine Stew
- Slow-Cooked Polenta with Roasted Tomatoes
- Slow-Cooked Italian Sausage and White Beans
- Slow-Cooked Gnocchi with Brown Butter and Sage
- Pollo al Chianti (Chicken in Chianti Wine Sauce)
- Slow-Cooked Italian Meatloaf with Parmesan
- Slow-Cooked Pork Loin with Garlic and Herbs
- Slow-Cooked Pumpkin and Sage Risotto
- Slow-Cooked Beef and Barley Soup

Classic Italian Beef Ragu

Ingredients

- 2 lbs beef chuck, cut into chunks
- 2 tbsp olive oil
- 1 onion, diced
- 2 carrots, diced
- 2 celery stalks, diced
- 4 garlic cloves, minced
- 1 cup red wine
- 1 can (28 oz) crushed tomatoes
- 1 cup beef broth
- 1 tbsp tomato paste
- 1 tsp dried oregano
- 1 tsp dried basil
- 1/2 tsp red pepper flakes (optional)
- Salt and pepper to taste
- Fresh parsley, chopped (for garnish)
- Cooked pasta of choice

Instructions

1. Heat olive oil in a large pot over medium-high heat. Add beef chunks and sear until browned on all sides. Remove and set aside.
2. In the same pot, add onion, carrots, celery, and garlic. Cook until softened, about 5 minutes.
3. Add red wine, scraping up any browned bits from the bottom of the pot. Simmer for 2 minutes.
4. Stir in crushed tomatoes, beef broth, tomato paste, oregano, basil, red pepper flakes, salt, and pepper. Return the beef to the pot.
5. Cover and simmer on low heat for 3-4 hours, until the beef is tender and shreds easily.
6. Shred the beef using two forks, stirring it into the sauce.
7. Serve over cooked pasta, garnished with fresh parsley.

Osso Buco alla Milanese

Ingredients

- 4 veal shanks, bone-in
- 2 tbsp olive oil
- 1 onion, chopped
- 2 carrots, chopped
- 2 celery stalks, chopped
- 4 garlic cloves, minced
- 1 cup white wine
- 1 can (14 oz) diced tomatoes
- 1 cup beef broth
- 1 tbsp tomato paste
- 2 sprigs fresh rosemary
- 2 sprigs fresh thyme
- 1/2 cup gremolata (lemon zest, garlic, and parsley mixture)
- Salt and pepper to taste
- Fresh parsley for garnish

Instructions

1. Heat olive oil in a large Dutch oven over medium-high heat. Brown the veal shanks on all sides and set aside.
2. Add onion, carrots, celery, and garlic to the pot. Cook until softened, about 5 minutes.
3. Add white wine, scraping up any browned bits from the bottom of the pot. Simmer for 2 minutes.
4. Stir in tomatoes, beef broth, tomato paste, rosemary, and thyme. Return the veal shanks to the pot.
5. Cover and simmer on low heat for 2-3 hours, until the meat is tender and falling off the bone.
6. Serve with a sprinkle of gremolata and garnish with fresh parsley.

Slow-Cooked Lasagna

Ingredients

- 12 lasagna noodles, uncooked
- 1 lb ground beef
- 1 onion, chopped
- 2 garlic cloves, minced
- 1 can (28 oz) crushed tomatoes
- 1 can (6 oz) tomato paste
- 2 tbsp tomato sauce
- 1 tbsp dried basil
- 1 tbsp dried oregano
- Salt and pepper to taste
- 16 oz ricotta cheese
- 3 cups shredded mozzarella cheese
- 1/2 cup grated Parmesan cheese
- Fresh basil for garnish

Instructions

1. In a skillet, cook ground beef and onion over medium heat until browned. Add garlic and cook for another minute.
2. Stir in crushed tomatoes, tomato paste, tomato sauce, basil, oregano, salt, and pepper. Simmer for 15-20 minutes.
3. In a mixing bowl, combine ricotta, 2 cups mozzarella, and Parmesan cheese.
4. In a slow cooker, layer the ingredients: start with a layer of meat sauce, followed by a layer of uncooked lasagna noodles, and then a layer of cheese mixture. Repeat until all ingredients are used.
5. Cover and cook on low for 4-6 hours, or until the noodles are tender and the cheese is melted.
6. Garnish with fresh basil before serving.

Italian Braised Short Ribs

Ingredients

- 4 beef short ribs
- 2 tbsp olive oil
- 1 onion, chopped
- 2 carrots, chopped
- 2 celery stalks, chopped
- 4 garlic cloves, minced
- 1 cup red wine
- 1 can (28 oz) crushed tomatoes
- 1 cup beef broth
- 2 sprigs fresh rosemary
- 2 sprigs fresh thyme
- Salt and pepper to taste

Instructions

1. Heat olive oil in a large Dutch oven over medium-high heat. Brown short ribs on all sides, then remove and set aside.
2. Add onion, carrots, celery, and garlic to the pot. Cook until softened, about 5 minutes.
3. Add red wine, scraping up any browned bits from the bottom. Simmer for 2 minutes.
4. Stir in crushed tomatoes, beef broth, rosemary, thyme, salt, and pepper. Return the short ribs to the pot.
5. Cover and cook on low heat for 3-4 hours, until the meat is tender and easily falls off the bone.
6. Serve the short ribs with the braising sauce.

Chicken Cacciatore

Ingredients

- 4 chicken thighs, bone-in, skinless
- 2 tbsp olive oil
- 1 onion, chopped
- 2 garlic cloves, minced
- 1 bell pepper, chopped
- 1 can (14 oz) diced tomatoes
- 1/2 cup white wine
- 1 cup chicken broth
- 1 tbsp capers
- 1 tbsp fresh oregano, chopped
- Salt and pepper to taste
- Fresh parsley for garnish

Instructions

1. Heat olive oil in a large skillet over medium-high heat. Brown the chicken thighs on both sides, then remove and set aside.
2. Add onion, garlic, and bell pepper to the skillet. Cook until softened, about 5 minutes.
3. Stir in diced tomatoes, white wine, chicken broth, capers, oregano, salt, and pepper.
4. Return the chicken to the skillet and simmer on low for 40-50 minutes, until the chicken is cooked through and tender.
5. Garnish with fresh parsley before serving.

Polenta with Slow-Cooked Mushrooms

Ingredients

- 1 cup polenta
- 4 cups vegetable broth
- 2 tbsp butter
- 2 tbsp olive oil
- 1 lb mixed mushrooms (cremini, shiitake, and portobello), sliced
- 2 garlic cloves, minced
- 1/4 cup white wine
- 1 tbsp fresh thyme, chopped
- Salt and pepper to taste
- Fresh Parmesan cheese, grated (for garnish)

Instructions

1. In a saucepan, bring vegetable broth to a boil. Slowly whisk in the polenta and reduce heat to low. Stir frequently until thickened, about 30 minutes. Stir in butter and season with salt and pepper.
2. While the polenta cooks, heat olive oil in a skillet over medium heat. Add mushrooms and garlic, and cook until softened, about 10 minutes.
3. Add white wine and thyme to the mushrooms. Simmer for 5 minutes, then season with salt and pepper.
4. Serve the polenta topped with the mushroom mixture, garnished with grated Parmesan.

Tuscan Bean and Sausage Stew

Ingredients

- 1 lb Italian sausage (bulk or casings removed)
- 1 onion, chopped
- 2 garlic cloves, minced
- 2 cans (15 oz each) cannellini beans, drained and rinsed
- 1 can (14 oz) diced tomatoes
- 4 cups chicken broth
- 2 cups kale, chopped
- 1 tsp dried thyme
- 1 tbsp fresh rosemary, chopped
- Salt and pepper to taste

Instructions

1. In a large pot, brown the sausage over medium heat, breaking it up into small pieces. Remove and set aside.
2. Add onion and garlic to the pot, cooking until softened.
3. Stir in the beans, diced tomatoes, chicken broth, thyme, rosemary, salt, and pepper.
4. Add the sausage back into the pot. Bring to a simmer and cook for 30 minutes.
5. Stir in the kale and cook for an additional 10 minutes, until tender.
6. Serve hot, garnished with fresh rosemary.

Italian Meatballs in Tomato Sauce

Ingredients

- 1 lb ground beef
- 1/2 lb ground pork
- 1/2 cup breadcrumbs
- 1/4 cup grated Parmesan cheese
- 1 egg
- 2 garlic cloves, minced
- 1 tbsp fresh parsley, chopped
- 1 tsp dried oregano
- 1 tsp salt
- 1/2 tsp pepper
- 1 can (28 oz) crushed tomatoes
- 1 tbsp olive oil
- 1 tsp sugar
- Fresh basil for garnish

Instructions

1. In a large bowl, mix together beef, pork, breadcrumbs, Parmesan, egg, garlic, parsley, oregano, salt, and pepper. Shape into meatballs.
2. Heat olive oil in a large skillet over medium heat. Brown the meatballs on all sides, then remove and set aside.
3. In the same skillet, add crushed tomatoes and sugar, stirring to combine.
4. Return the meatballs to the skillet, simmering in the sauce for 30 minutes, until cooked through.
5. Serve the meatballs with the sauce and garnish with fresh basil.

Slow-Cooked Porchetta

Ingredients

- 4-5 lb pork belly, with skin on
- 2 tbsp olive oil
- 2 tbsp fresh rosemary, chopped
- 4 garlic cloves, minced
- 1 tbsp fennel seeds, crushed
- 1 tsp salt
- 1/2 tsp black pepper
- Zest of 1 lemon
- 1 cup white wine
- 1 cup chicken broth

Instructions

1. Preheat oven to 300°F (150°C).
2. In a small bowl, mix rosemary, garlic, fennel seeds, lemon zest, salt, and pepper. Rub this mixture all over the pork belly.
3. Heat olive oil in a large skillet over medium-high heat. Sear the pork belly on all sides until golden brown.
4. Transfer the pork to a slow cooker. Add white wine and chicken broth to the slow cooker.
5. Cover and cook on low for 6-8 hours, until the pork is tender and the skin is crispy.
6. Remove from the slow cooker, slice, and serve with the juices from the cooker.

Vitello Tonato (Veal with Tuna Sauce)

Ingredients

- 2 lb veal roast
- 2 tbsp olive oil
- 1 onion, halved
- 2 celery stalks, halved
- 2 carrots, halved
- 1 bay leaf
- 2 cups white wine
- 1/2 cup water
- 1 jar (6 oz) tuna packed in olive oil
- 2 tbsp capers
- 2 tbsp mayonnaise
- 1 tbsp Dijon mustard
- 1 tbsp lemon juice
- Salt and pepper to taste
- Fresh parsley for garnish

Instructions

1. Preheat oven to 350°F (175°C).
2. In a large roasting pan, heat olive oil over medium-high heat. Brown the veal on all sides.
3. Add the onion, celery, carrots, and bay leaf to the pan. Pour in white wine and water. Cover with foil and roast for 1.5 hours, until the veal is tender.
4. While the veal roasts, combine tuna, capers, mayonnaise, mustard, lemon juice, salt, and pepper in a food processor. Blend until smooth.
5. Once the veal is cooked, let it rest. Slice the veal thinly and serve topped with the tuna sauce. Garnish with fresh parsley.

Risotto alla Milanese

Ingredients

- 1 1/2 cups Arborio rice
- 4 cups chicken broth
- 1/2 cup dry white wine
- 1 small onion, finely chopped
- 2 tbsp olive oil
- 2 tbsp butter
- 1/2 tsp saffron threads
- 1/2 cup grated Parmesan cheese
- Salt and pepper to taste

Instructions

1. In a small saucepan, heat the chicken broth and add saffron. Keep warm.
2. In a large pan, heat olive oil and butter over medium heat. Add chopped onion and sauté until softened.
3. Add the rice to the pan and cook for 2 minutes, stirring constantly.
4. Pour in the white wine and cook until absorbed. Begin adding the saffron-infused broth, one ladle at a time, stirring constantly until the liquid is absorbed before adding more.
5. Continue adding broth and stirring for about 18-20 minutes, until the rice is creamy and tender.
6. Stir in the Parmesan, salt, and pepper. Serve hot.

Slow-Cooked Bolognese Sauce

Ingredients

- 1 lb ground beef
- 1 lb ground pork
- 1 onion, chopped
- 2 carrots, chopped
- 2 celery stalks, chopped
- 4 garlic cloves, minced
- 1 cup red wine
- 1 can (28 oz) crushed tomatoes
- 1/4 cup tomato paste
- 1/2 cup whole milk
- 2 tbsp olive oil
- 1 tsp dried oregano
- 1 tsp dried basil
- Salt and pepper to taste

Instructions

1. In a large skillet, heat olive oil over medium-high heat. Brown the beef and pork, breaking it up with a spoon.
2. Add onion, carrots, celery, and garlic. Cook until softened, about 5 minutes.
3. Stir in red wine and cook for 2 minutes, scraping up any browned bits.
4. Transfer the mixture to a slow cooker. Add crushed tomatoes, tomato paste, milk, oregano, basil, salt, and pepper.
5. Cover and cook on low for 6-8 hours, stirring occasionally. Serve over pasta.

Stracciatella Soup (Italian Egg Drop Soup)

Ingredients

- 4 cups chicken broth
- 2 eggs
- 1/4 cup grated Parmesan cheese
- 1 tbsp fresh parsley, chopped
- Salt and pepper to taste

Instructions

1. Bring the chicken broth to a simmer in a pot.
2. In a small bowl, beat the eggs with Parmesan, salt, and pepper.
3. Slowly pour the egg mixture into the simmering broth in a thin stream, stirring constantly to create ribbons of egg.
4. Continue to cook for 2-3 minutes until the egg is fully cooked.
5. Garnish with fresh parsley and serve hot.

Slow-Cooked Eggplant Parmesan

Ingredients

- 2 large eggplants, sliced into 1/2-inch rounds
- 2 cups marinara sauce
- 2 cups shredded mozzarella cheese
- 1/2 cup grated Parmesan cheese
- 1 cup breadcrumbs
- 1/4 cup fresh basil, chopped
- 2 tbsp olive oil
- Salt and pepper to taste

Instructions

1. Preheat oven to 375°F (190°C).
2. Arrange eggplant slices on a baking sheet. Drizzle with olive oil, and season with salt and pepper. Roast in the oven for 20 minutes.
3. In a slow cooker, layer marinara sauce, roasted eggplant, mozzarella, Parmesan, and breadcrumbs.
4. Continue layering until all ingredients are used.
5. Cover and cook on low for 4-5 hours, until the cheese is melted and bubbly.
6. Garnish with fresh basil and serve.

Osso Buco with Risotto

Ingredients

- 4 veal shanks, bone-in
- 2 tbsp olive oil
- 1 onion, chopped
- 2 carrots, chopped
- 2 celery stalks, chopped
- 4 garlic cloves, minced
- 1 cup white wine
- 2 cups chicken broth
- 1 can (14 oz) diced tomatoes
- 2 sprigs fresh rosemary
- 1/2 cup gremolata (lemon zest, garlic, and parsley mixture)
- Salt and pepper to taste
- 1 1/2 cups Arborio rice (for risotto)
- 4 cups chicken broth (for risotto)
- 1/2 cup Parmesan cheese (for risotto)

Instructions

1. In a large Dutch oven, heat olive oil over medium-high heat. Brown veal shanks on all sides.
2. Add onion, carrots, celery, and garlic to the pot. Cook for 5 minutes.
3. Stir in white wine and cook for 2 minutes. Add chicken broth, diced tomatoes, rosemary, salt, and pepper.
4. Cover and cook for 2-3 hours, until the veal is tender.
5. For the risotto, bring chicken broth to a simmer in a separate pot. In another pan, heat olive oil and add Arborio rice. Cook for 2 minutes.
6. Gradually add the warm chicken broth, stirring constantly until absorbed, until the rice is creamy and tender.
7. Stir in Parmesan cheese and season with salt and pepper.
8. Serve osso buco with risotto and garnish with gremolata.

Zuppa Toscana (Tuscan Soup)

Ingredients

- 1 lb Italian sausage
- 4 large russet potatoes, sliced
- 1 onion, chopped
- 4 garlic cloves, minced
- 4 cups chicken broth
- 2 cups kale, chopped
- 1 cup heavy cream
- 1/2 tsp red pepper flakes
- Salt and pepper to taste

Instructions

1. In a large pot, cook Italian sausage over medium heat until browned.
2. Add onion and garlic, cooking until softened.
3. Add chicken broth, potatoes, and red pepper flakes. Bring to a boil, then reduce heat and simmer for 20 minutes, until potatoes are tender.
4. Stir in kale and cook for 5 minutes.
5. Add heavy cream, salt, and pepper. Simmer for an additional 5 minutes.
6. Serve hot, garnished with extra kale if desired.

Slow-Cooked Italian Sausage and Peppers

Ingredients

- 4 Italian sausages (sweet or spicy)
- 2 bell peppers, sliced
- 1 onion, sliced
- 4 garlic cloves, minced
- 1 can (14 oz) crushed tomatoes
- 1 tsp dried oregano
- 1 tsp red pepper flakes (optional)
- Salt and pepper to taste
- 1/4 cup fresh basil, chopped
- 1/4 cup olive oil

Instructions

1. Heat olive oil in a skillet over medium heat. Brown sausages on all sides, then transfer them to the slow cooker.
2. In the same skillet, sauté onions, peppers, and garlic until softened, about 5 minutes. Add to the slow cooker with the crushed tomatoes, oregano, red pepper flakes, salt, and pepper.
3. Cover and cook on low for 6-8 hours, until the sausages are tender.
4. Serve with fresh basil sprinkled on top, and enjoy over pasta, rice, or in a sandwich.

Gnocchi with Slow-Cooked Pork Ragu

Ingredients

- 1 lb pork shoulder, boneless
- 2 tbsp olive oil
- 1 onion, chopped
- 2 carrots, chopped
- 2 celery stalks, chopped
- 3 garlic cloves, minced
- 1 cup dry white wine
- 2 cups crushed tomatoes
- 1 tsp dried thyme
- 1 tsp dried oregano
- Salt and pepper to taste
- 1 lb potato gnocchi, cooked
- 1/4 cup fresh parsley, chopped
- 1/4 cup grated Parmesan cheese

Instructions

1. Heat olive oil in a large skillet over medium-high heat. Brown the pork on all sides, then transfer to the slow cooker.
2. In the same skillet, sauté onion, carrots, celery, and garlic until softened, about 5 minutes. Add to the slow cooker with wine, tomatoes, thyme, oregano, salt, and pepper.
3. Cover and cook on low for 6-8 hours, until the pork is tender and easily shreds.
4. Shred the pork in the slow cooker and stir. Serve over cooked gnocchi, garnished with fresh parsley and Parmesan cheese.

Slow-Cooked Veal Piccata

Ingredients

- 4 veal cutlets
- 2 tbsp olive oil
- 1 onion, chopped
- 2 garlic cloves, minced
- 1/2 cup white wine
- 2 cups chicken broth
- 1/4 cup fresh lemon juice
- 2 tbsp capers
- 1/4 cup fresh parsley, chopped
- Salt and pepper to taste

Instructions

1. Heat olive oil in a skillet over medium-high heat. Brown veal cutlets on both sides, then transfer to the slow cooker.
2. In the same skillet, sauté onion and garlic until softened, about 3 minutes. Add wine and bring to a simmer, scraping up any browned bits from the skillet. Pour into the slow cooker.
3. Add chicken broth, lemon juice, capers, salt, and pepper to the slow cooker.
4. Cover and cook on low for 3-4 hours, until the veal is tender.
5. Garnish with fresh parsley and serve with pasta or potatoes.

Beef Braciole

Ingredients

- 4 beef flank steaks, pounded thin
- 1/2 cup breadcrumbs
- 1/4 cup grated Parmesan cheese
- 2 garlic cloves, minced
- 1/4 cup fresh parsley, chopped
- 1/4 cup olive oil
- 1 can (14 oz) crushed tomatoes
- 1 cup red wine
- 1 tsp dried basil
- Salt and pepper to taste

Instructions

1. Lay the flank steaks flat and season both sides with salt and pepper. In a bowl, combine breadcrumbs, Parmesan, garlic, and parsley.
2. Spread the breadcrumb mixture over each steak, then roll them up and secure with toothpicks.
3. Heat olive oil in a skillet over medium-high heat. Brown the braciole on all sides, then transfer to the slow cooker.
4. Pour crushed tomatoes and red wine over the braciole, then add basil, salt, and pepper.
5. Cover and cook on low for 6-8 hours, until the beef is tender. Serve with pasta or crusty bread.

Pasta Fagioli

Ingredients

- 1 lb dried cannellini beans, soaked overnight
- 2 tbsp olive oil
- 1 onion, chopped
- 2 garlic cloves, minced
- 2 carrots, chopped
- 2 celery stalks, chopped
- 1 can (14 oz) diced tomatoes
- 1 tsp dried rosemary
- 1 tsp dried thyme
- 6 cups vegetable broth
- 1 cup small pasta (e.g., ditalini or elbow macaroni)
- Salt and pepper to taste
- 1/4 cup fresh basil, chopped

Instructions

1. In a large pot, heat olive oil over medium heat. Sauté onion, garlic, carrots, and celery until softened, about 5 minutes.
2. Add soaked beans, diced tomatoes, rosemary, thyme, and vegetable broth to the slow cooker.
3. Cover and cook on low for 6-8 hours, until the beans are tender.
4. About 30 minutes before serving, add pasta to the slow cooker and cook until tender.
5. Season with salt and pepper, and garnish with fresh basil before serving.

Slow-Cooked Lamb Shanks with Garlic and Rosemary

Ingredients

- 4 lamb shanks
- 2 tbsp olive oil
- 4 garlic cloves, minced
- 2 sprigs fresh rosemary
- 2 cups red wine
- 2 cups beef broth
- 1 onion, chopped
- 2 carrots, chopped
- Salt and pepper to taste

Instructions

1. Heat olive oil in a large skillet over medium-high heat. Brown the lamb shanks on all sides, then transfer to the slow cooker.
2. In the same skillet, sauté garlic, onion, and carrots for 5 minutes. Add wine, beef broth, rosemary, salt, and pepper.
3. Pour the mixture over the lamb shanks in the slow cooker.
4. Cover and cook on low for 7-8 hours, until the lamb is tender and falling off the bone.
5. Serve with mashed potatoes or rice, and garnish with fresh rosemary.

Slow-Cooked Pollo alla Romana

Ingredients

- 4 bone-in chicken thighs
- 1 onion, chopped
- 4 garlic cloves, minced
- 1/2 cup white wine
- 2 cups crushed tomatoes
- 1 tsp dried oregano
- 1 tsp dried basil
- 1/2 tsp red pepper flakes
- Salt and pepper to taste
- 1/4 cup fresh parsley, chopped

Instructions

1. Heat olive oil in a skillet over medium heat. Brown chicken thighs on both sides, then transfer to the slow cooker.
2. In the same skillet, sauté onion and garlic for 3 minutes. Add wine and bring to a simmer, then pour into the slow cooker.
3. Add crushed tomatoes, oregano, basil, red pepper flakes, salt, and pepper to the slow cooker.
4. Cover and cook on low for 6-7 hours, until the chicken is cooked through and tender.
5. Garnish with fresh parsley before serving, and enjoy with crusty bread or pasta.

Slow-Braised Capon

Ingredients

- 1 capon (about 4-5 lb), cleaned and trussed
- 2 tbsp olive oil
- 1 onion, chopped
- 2 carrots, chopped
- 2 celery stalks, chopped
- 4 garlic cloves, minced
- 2 cups white wine
- 2 cups chicken broth
- 1 tsp dried thyme
- 2 sprigs fresh rosemary
- Salt and pepper to taste

Instructions

1. Preheat the oven to 325°F (165°C).
2. Heat olive oil in a large skillet over medium-high heat. Brown the capon on all sides, then transfer to a roasting pan or slow cooker.
3. In the same skillet, sauté onion, carrots, celery, and garlic for 5 minutes. Add white wine, chicken broth, thyme, rosemary, salt, and pepper.
4. Pour the mixture over the capon.
5. Cover and cook in the oven for 3-4 hours, or cook on low in the slow cooker for 6-8 hours, until the capon is tender and fully cooked.
6. Serve with roasted vegetables or mashed potatoes.

Italian-Inspired Slow-Cooked Pork Roast

Ingredients

- 4-5 lb pork roast (shoulder or butt)
- 2 tbsp olive oil
- 4 garlic cloves, minced
- 2 tbsp fresh rosemary, chopped
- 1 tbsp fresh thyme, chopped
- 1 tsp dried oregano
- 1 cup dry white wine
- 2 cups chicken broth
- 2 tbsp balsamic vinegar
- Salt and pepper to taste
- 1 onion, sliced
- 1 carrot, chopped
- 1 celery stalk, chopped

Instructions

1. Rub the pork roast with olive oil, garlic, rosemary, thyme, oregano, salt, and pepper.
2. Heat a skillet over medium-high heat and brown the roast on all sides. Transfer to the slow cooker.
3. In the same skillet, sauté the onion, carrot, and celery for 5 minutes. Add the wine, chicken broth, and balsamic vinegar, scraping up any browned bits. Pour the mixture over the roast in the slow cooker.
4. Cover and cook on low for 6-8 hours, or until the pork is fork-tender.
5. Slice and serve with the cooking juices and roasted vegetables or mashed potatoes.

Stewed Chickpeas with Garlic and Herbs

Ingredients

- 2 cups dried chickpeas (or 4 cups canned chickpeas)
- 4 garlic cloves, minced
- 1 onion, chopped
- 2 cups vegetable broth
- 1 tsp dried thyme
- 1 tsp dried rosemary
- 1 bay leaf
- Salt and pepper to taste
- 2 tbsp olive oil
- 1/4 cup fresh parsley, chopped

Instructions

1. If using dried chickpeas, soak them overnight and drain.
2. In a large pot or slow cooker, heat olive oil over medium heat. Sauté garlic and onion until softened, about 5 minutes.
3. Add chickpeas, vegetable broth, thyme, rosemary, bay leaf, salt, and pepper. Stir to combine.
4. Cover and cook on low for 6-8 hours (or on the stovetop for 1-1.5 hours) until chickpeas are tender.
5. Garnish with fresh parsley and serve with crusty bread or over rice.

Slow-Cooked Risotto with Mushrooms

Ingredients

- 1 1/2 cups Arborio rice
- 4 cups vegetable or chicken broth
- 2 tbsp olive oil
- 1 onion, chopped
- 3 garlic cloves, minced
- 2 cups mushrooms (such as cremini or button), sliced
- 1/2 cup dry white wine
- 1/4 cup Parmesan cheese, grated
- 2 tbsp butter
- Salt and pepper to taste
- Fresh parsley, chopped for garnish

Instructions

1. Heat olive oil in a skillet over medium heat. Sauté the onion and garlic for 5 minutes until softened. Add the mushrooms and cook until tender.
2. Transfer the mixture to the slow cooker, then add the Arborio rice, broth, and white wine. Stir to combine.
3. Cover and cook on low for 2-3 hours, stirring occasionally, until the rice is tender and creamy.
4. Stir in Parmesan cheese and butter, then season with salt and pepper.
5. Garnish with fresh parsley and serve.

Slow-Cooked Risotto alla Milanese with Saffron

Ingredients

- 1 1/2 cups Arborio rice
- 4 cups chicken broth
- 1/4 tsp saffron threads
- 1/2 cup dry white wine
- 1 onion, chopped
- 2 tbsp olive oil
- 1/4 cup grated Parmesan cheese
- 2 tbsp butter
- Salt and pepper to taste

Instructions

1. Heat the chicken broth in a small saucepan and add the saffron threads. Let steep for 10 minutes.
2. In a skillet, sauté the onion in olive oil over medium heat for 5 minutes.
3. Transfer the onion to the slow cooker and add the Arborio rice, saffron-infused broth, and white wine. Stir to combine.
4. Cover and cook on low for 2-3 hours, stirring occasionally, until the rice is tender and creamy.
5. Stir in Parmesan cheese and butter. Season with salt and pepper before serving.

Frittata di Patate (Potato Frittata)

Ingredients

- 6 large eggs
- 2 cups cooked potatoes, sliced or diced
- 1 onion, thinly sliced
- 1/2 cup Parmesan cheese, grated
- 1/2 cup milk
- 2 tbsp olive oil
- Salt and pepper to taste
- Fresh parsley, chopped for garnish

Instructions

1. Heat olive oil in a skillet over medium heat. Sauté the onion until softened, about 5 minutes. Add the cooked potatoes and cook until lightly golden.
2. In a bowl, whisk together eggs, milk, Parmesan cheese, salt, and pepper. Pour over the potato mixture.
3. Lower the heat and cook until the edges are set, about 10-12 minutes.
4. Transfer the skillet to a preheated broiler and cook for 3-4 minutes until the top is golden and firm.
5. Garnish with fresh parsley and serve warm or at room temperature.

Pasta alla Norma (Eggplant and Ricotta)

Ingredients

- 2 medium eggplants, diced
- 1 lb pasta (spaghetti, rigatoni, or penne)
- 3 cups crushed tomatoes
- 2 garlic cloves, minced
- 1/2 cup fresh ricotta cheese
- 1/4 cup fresh basil, chopped
- 1/4 cup olive oil
- Salt and pepper to taste

Instructions

1. Heat olive oil in a large skillet over medium heat. Sauté the eggplant in batches until tender and lightly browned, about 5-7 minutes.
2. Remove the eggplant and set aside. In the same skillet, sauté garlic for 1 minute, then add the crushed tomatoes.
3. Simmer for 10 minutes, then add the eggplant back to the skillet. Season with salt and pepper.
4. Cook the pasta according to package instructions. Drain and toss with the tomato and eggplant sauce.
5. Top with fresh ricotta and basil before serving.

Minestrone Soup

Ingredients

- 2 tbsp olive oil
- 1 onion, chopped
- 2 garlic cloves, minced
- 2 carrots, chopped
- 2 celery stalks, chopped
- 2 potatoes, peeled and diced
- 1 zucchini, chopped
- 1 can (14 oz) diced tomatoes
- 1 can (15 oz) cannellini beans, drained
- 6 cups vegetable broth
- 1 cup pasta (small shapes like ditalini or elbow)
- 1 tsp dried thyme
- Salt and pepper to taste
- Fresh parsley for garnish

Instructions

1. Heat olive oil in a large pot over medium heat. Sauté the onion, garlic, carrots, celery, and potatoes for 5 minutes.
2. Add the zucchini, tomatoes, beans, vegetable broth, and thyme. Bring to a simmer.
3. Cover and cook on low for 1 hour, until the vegetables are tender.
4. Add the pasta and cook for an additional 15-20 minutes.
5. Season with salt and pepper, and garnish with fresh parsley before serving.

Slow-Cooked Goulash with Italian Sausage

Ingredients

- 1 lb Italian sausage (sweet or spicy), removed from casings
- 1 onion, chopped
- 2 garlic cloves, minced
- 2 cups beef broth
- 1 can (14 oz) diced tomatoes
- 1 tbsp paprika
- 1 tsp dried oregano
- 1/2 cup heavy cream
- 1/4 cup grated Parmesan cheese
- Salt and pepper to taste
- 1 lb elbow macaroni or other small pasta

Instructions

1. In a skillet, brown the Italian sausage with onion and garlic over medium-high heat, breaking up the sausage into small crumbles.
2. Transfer the sausage mixture to the slow cooker. Add beef broth, diced tomatoes, paprika, oregano, salt, and pepper.
3. Cover and cook on low for 4-6 hours, until the sausage is tender.
4. About 30 minutes before serving, cook the pasta according to package instructions.
5. Stir in the cream and Parmesan cheese into the slow cooker, then add the cooked pasta. Serve warm.

Italian-American Chicken Parmigiana

Ingredients

- 4 boneless, skinless chicken breasts
- 1 cup all-purpose flour
- 2 large eggs, beaten
- 1 1/2 cups breadcrumbs
- 1/2 cup grated Parmesan cheese
- 1 cup marinara sauce
- 1 1/2 cups mozzarella cheese, shredded
- 2 tbsp olive oil
- Salt and pepper to taste
- Fresh basil leaves for garnish

Instructions

1. Preheat the oven to 375°F (190°C).
2. Season the chicken breasts with salt and pepper. Dredge them in flour, dip in beaten eggs, then coat with a mixture of breadcrumbs and Parmesan cheese.
3. Heat olive oil in a skillet over medium heat. Brown the chicken on both sides, about 4 minutes per side.
4. Place the chicken on a baking dish, and top each with marinara sauce and mozzarella.
5. Bake for 20-25 minutes until the chicken is cooked through and the cheese is bubbly and golden.
6. Garnish with fresh basil before serving.

Slow-Cooked Ziti with Sausage and Cheese

Ingredients

- 1 lb ziti pasta
- 1 lb Italian sausage (sweet or spicy), crumbled
- 1 onion, chopped
- 2 garlic cloves, minced
- 1 can (28 oz) crushed tomatoes
- 1 tbsp dried oregano
- 1 tbsp dried basil
- 1/2 tsp red pepper flakes (optional)
- 2 cups ricotta cheese
- 1 1/2 cups mozzarella cheese, shredded
- 1/2 cup Parmesan cheese, grated
- Salt and pepper to taste
- Fresh basil for garnish

Instructions

1. Cook ziti pasta according to package directions, drain, and set aside.
2. In a skillet, brown the sausage over medium heat. Add the onion and garlic and cook until softened, about 5 minutes.
3. Add crushed tomatoes, oregano, basil, red pepper flakes, salt, and pepper. Simmer for 10 minutes.
4. In a slow cooker, layer the pasta, sausage mixture, ricotta cheese, mozzarella, and Parmesan. Repeat the layers.
5. Cover and cook on low for 4 hours, or until the cheese is melted and bubbly.
6. Garnish with fresh basil before serving.

Ribollita (Tuscan Bread Soup)

Ingredients

- 2 tbsp olive oil
- 1 onion, chopped
- 2 carrots, chopped
- 2 celery stalks, chopped
- 4 garlic cloves, minced
- 1 can (14 oz) diced tomatoes
- 6 cups vegetable broth
- 4 cups kale, chopped
- 4 cups day-old bread, torn into pieces
- 1 tsp dried thyme
- 1 tsp dried rosemary
- Salt and pepper to taste
- Fresh Parmesan cheese for garnish

Instructions

1. Heat olive oil in a large pot over medium heat. Sauté the onion, carrots, celery, and garlic until softened, about 7 minutes.
2. Add the diced tomatoes, vegetable broth, kale, thyme, rosemary, salt, and pepper. Bring to a boil.
3. Reduce the heat and simmer for 20 minutes.
4. Stir in the torn bread and cook for an additional 10-15 minutes, until the bread breaks down and thickens the soup.
5. Serve topped with fresh Parmesan cheese.

Slow-Cooked Tomato and Basil Soup

Ingredients

- 2 tbsp olive oil
- 1 onion, chopped
- 4 garlic cloves, minced
- 6 cups canned whole tomatoes, crushed
- 1 1/2 cups vegetable broth
- 1 tbsp dried basil
- 1 tsp sugar (optional)
- Salt and pepper to taste
- 1/2 cup heavy cream
- Fresh basil leaves for garnish

Instructions

1. Heat olive oil in a large pot over medium heat. Sauté the onion and garlic until softened, about 5 minutes.
2. Add crushed tomatoes, vegetable broth, basil, sugar, salt, and pepper. Bring to a boil.
3. Reduce the heat and simmer for 20 minutes.
4. Use an immersion blender to puree the soup until smooth.
5. Stir in the heavy cream and adjust seasoning as needed.
6. Serve garnished with fresh basil leaves.

Slow-Cooked Pappardelle with Wild Boar Ragu

Ingredients

- 1 lb wild boar shoulder, cubed
- 2 tbsp olive oil
- 1 onion, chopped
- 2 garlic cloves, minced
- 1 cup red wine
- 1 can (14 oz) crushed tomatoes
- 1 tbsp dried oregano
- 1 tsp dried thyme
- Salt and pepper to taste
- 1 lb pappardelle pasta
- 1/4 cup fresh parsley, chopped
- Fresh Parmesan cheese for garnish

Instructions

1. Heat olive oil in a skillet over medium-high heat. Brown the wild boar cubes on all sides, about 5 minutes.
2. Transfer the meat to a slow cooker. In the same skillet, sauté the onion and garlic for 5 minutes. Add the wine and let it reduce for 2 minutes.
3. Pour the onion and wine mixture into the slow cooker with the wild boar. Add crushed tomatoes, oregano, thyme, salt, and pepper.
4. Cover and cook on low for 6-8 hours, until the meat is tender.
5. Cook pappardelle pasta according to package instructions.
6. Toss the cooked pasta with the ragu and serve garnished with fresh parsley and Parmesan cheese.

Pork Saltimbocca

Ingredients

- 4 pork chops (or pork cutlets)
- 8 slices prosciutto
- 8 fresh sage leaves
- 1 tbsp olive oil
- 1/2 cup white wine
- 1/2 cup chicken broth
- 1 tbsp butter
- Salt and pepper to taste

Instructions

1. Season the pork with salt and pepper. Place a slice of prosciutto and a sage leaf on each piece of pork, then secure with toothpicks.
2. Heat olive oil in a large skillet over medium-high heat. Brown the pork on both sides, about 4 minutes per side.
3. Remove the pork from the skillet and set aside. Add white wine and chicken broth, scraping up any browned bits from the pan.
4. Return the pork to the skillet and simmer in the sauce for 10 minutes, until the sauce reduces slightly.
5. Stir in the butter and serve.

Slow-Cooked Sicilian Meatloaf

Ingredients

- 1 lb ground beef
- 1 lb ground pork
- 1 cup breadcrumbs
- 1/2 cup grated Parmesan cheese
- 2 large eggs, beaten
- 1 onion, chopped
- 3 garlic cloves, minced
- 1/2 cup milk
- 1/4 cup fresh parsley, chopped
- 1 can (14 oz) crushed tomatoes
- 1 tbsp dried oregano
- Salt and pepper to taste

Instructions

1. In a large bowl, mix together ground beef, ground pork, breadcrumbs, Parmesan, eggs, onion, garlic, milk, parsley, salt, and pepper.
2. Shape the mixture into a loaf and place it in the slow cooker.
3. Pour crushed tomatoes over the meatloaf and sprinkle with oregano.
4. Cover and cook on low for 6-8 hours.
5. Slice and serve with additional sauce from the slow cooker.

Braised Fennel with Parmesan

Ingredients

- 2 large fennel bulbs, sliced
- 2 tbsp olive oil
- 1 cup vegetable broth
- 1/2 cup grated Parmesan cheese
- Salt and pepper to taste

Instructions

1. Heat olive oil in a large skillet over medium heat. Add fennel slices and sauté for 5 minutes until golden.
2. Add vegetable broth, salt, and pepper. Cover and simmer for 20 minutes, until fennel is tender.
3. Top with grated Parmesan cheese and serve.

Italian Style Braised Brussels Sprouts

Ingredients

- 1 lb Brussels sprouts, trimmed and halved
- 2 tbsp olive oil
- 3 garlic cloves, minced
- 1/2 cup vegetable broth
- 1/2 tsp red pepper flakes (optional)
- Salt and pepper to taste
- 1/4 cup fresh Parmesan cheese, grated

Instructions

1. Heat olive oil in a skillet over medium-high heat. Add Brussels sprouts and sauté until browned, about 7 minutes.
2. Add garlic and cook for 1 minute.
3. Pour in vegetable broth, red pepper flakes, salt, and pepper. Cover and braise for 15-20 minutes until tender.
4. Top with grated Parmesan cheese and serve.

Slow-Cooked Beef and Red Wine Stew

Ingredients

- 2 lbs beef stew meat, cut into cubes
- 2 tbsp olive oil
- 1 onion, chopped
- 2 carrots, chopped
- 3 garlic cloves, minced
- 1 cup red wine
- 4 cups beef broth
- 1 tbsp dried thyme
- 1 bay leaf
- 1 tbsp tomato paste
- Salt and pepper to taste
- 2 tbsp fresh parsley, chopped (for garnish)

Instructions

1. Heat olive oil in a large skillet over medium-high heat. Brown the beef stew meat on all sides, about 5 minutes.
2. Transfer the browned beef to a slow cooker.
3. In the same skillet, sauté the onion, carrots, and garlic for 5 minutes until softened.
4. Add the tomato paste and cook for another minute.
5. Pour in the red wine to deglaze the skillet, scraping up any browned bits from the bottom.
6. Transfer the mixture to the slow cooker with the beef. Add the beef broth, thyme, bay leaf, salt, and pepper.
7. Cover and cook on low for 7-8 hours, until the beef is tender.
8. Remove the bay leaf, and garnish with fresh parsley before serving.

Slow-Cooked Polenta with Roasted Tomatoes

Ingredients

- 1 cup polenta (cornmeal)
- 4 cups vegetable broth
- 1 tbsp olive oil
- 1 tsp garlic powder
- 1 tsp dried thyme
- Salt and pepper to taste
- 2 cups cherry tomatoes, halved
- 1 tbsp balsamic vinegar
- 1 tbsp olive oil (for roasting)
- Fresh basil for garnish

Instructions

1. In a slow cooker, combine the polenta, vegetable broth, olive oil, garlic powder, thyme, salt, and pepper. Stir to combine.
2. Cover and cook on low for 4-6 hours, stirring occasionally, until the polenta is thick and creamy.
3. While the polenta cooks, preheat the oven to 400°F (200°C).
4. Toss the cherry tomatoes with balsamic vinegar, olive oil, salt, and pepper.
5. Spread the tomatoes on a baking sheet and roast for 20-25 minutes, until soft and slightly caramelized.
6. Once the polenta is ready, top it with the roasted tomatoes and garnish with fresh basil before serving.

Slow-Cooked Italian Sausage and White Beans

Ingredients

- 1 lb Italian sausage (bulk or casing removed)
- 1 onion, chopped
- 2 garlic cloves, minced
- 2 cans (15 oz) white beans (such as cannellini or great northern), drained and rinsed
- 1 can (14 oz) diced tomatoes
- 1 tsp dried oregano
- 1 tsp dried basil
- 1/2 tsp red pepper flakes (optional)
- Salt and pepper to taste
- Fresh parsley for garnish

Instructions

1. Brown the sausage in a large skillet over medium heat until fully cooked, breaking it into crumbles as it cooks.
2. Transfer the cooked sausage to a slow cooker.
3. In the same skillet, sauté the onion and garlic for 5 minutes until softened.
4. Add the onion and garlic to the slow cooker along with the beans, diced tomatoes, oregano, basil, red pepper flakes, salt, and pepper.
5. Cover and cook on low for 6-8 hours, until the flavors have melded together.
6. Garnish with fresh parsley before serving.

Slow-Cooked Gnocchi with Brown Butter and Sage

Ingredients

- 1 lb potato gnocchi (store-bought or homemade)
- 4 tbsp unsalted butter
- 10-12 fresh sage leaves
- 1/4 cup grated Parmesan cheese
- Salt and pepper to taste
- Fresh parsley for garnish

Instructions

1. Cook the gnocchi according to package instructions, then drain and set aside.
2. In a skillet, melt the butter over medium heat. Cook until the butter turns golden brown and starts to smell nutty, about 5 minutes.
3. Add the sage leaves to the butter and cook for 1-2 minutes until crispy.
4. Transfer the cooked gnocchi to a slow cooker.
5. Pour the brown butter and sage mixture over the gnocchi, and stir to coat evenly.
6. Cover and cook on low for 2-3 hours.
7. Before serving, sprinkle with Parmesan cheese and garnish with fresh parsley.

Pollo al Chianti (Chicken in Chianti Wine Sauce)

Ingredients

- 4 chicken thighs, bone-in, skin-on
- 2 tbsp olive oil
- 1 onion, chopped
- 3 garlic cloves, minced
- 1 cup Chianti wine
- 1 cup chicken broth
- 1 tbsp tomato paste
- 1 tsp dried thyme
- 1 tsp dried rosemary
- Salt and pepper to taste
- Fresh parsley for garnish

Instructions

1. Heat olive oil in a large skillet over medium-high heat. Brown the chicken thighs on both sides for about 5 minutes.
2. Transfer the browned chicken to a slow cooker.
3. In the same skillet, sauté the onion and garlic for 5 minutes until softened.
4. Stir in the tomato paste, thyme, rosemary, salt, and pepper.
5. Pour in the Chianti wine and chicken broth, scraping up any browned bits from the bottom of the pan.
6. Pour the wine mixture over the chicken in the slow cooker.
7. Cover and cook on low for 6-8 hours until the chicken is tender.
8. Garnish with fresh parsley before serving.

Slow-Cooked Italian Meatloaf with Parmesan

Ingredients

- 1 lb ground beef
- 1/2 lb ground pork
- 1/2 cup breadcrumbs
- 1/4 cup grated Parmesan cheese
- 2 eggs
- 2 garlic cloves, minced
- 1/2 onion, finely chopped
- 1/4 cup milk
- 1 tsp dried oregano
- 1 tsp dried basil
- 1/2 tsp salt
- 1/4 tsp black pepper
- 1/4 cup marinara sauce (for topping)

Instructions

1. In a large mixing bowl, combine the ground beef, ground pork, breadcrumbs, Parmesan, eggs, garlic, onion, milk, oregano, basil, salt, and pepper.
2. Mix until everything is well incorporated.
3. Form the meat mixture into a loaf and place it in the slow cooker.
4. Spread marinara sauce over the top of the meatloaf.
5. Cover and cook on low for 6-8 hours, or until the meatloaf is fully cooked.
6. Slice and serve.

Slow-Cooked Pork Loin with Garlic and Herbs

Ingredients

- 2-3 lb pork loin
- 4 garlic cloves, minced
- 2 tbsp olive oil
- 1 tbsp fresh rosemary, chopped
- 1 tbsp fresh thyme, chopped
- 1 tsp salt
- 1/2 tsp black pepper
- 1/2 cup chicken broth
- 1 tbsp Dijon mustard

Instructions

1. Rub the pork loin with olive oil, garlic, rosemary, thyme, salt, and pepper.
2. Place the pork loin in the slow cooker and pour the chicken broth around the meat.
3. Spread Dijon mustard over the top of the pork.
4. Cover and cook on low for 7-8 hours until the pork is tender.
5. Slice the pork loin and serve with the cooking juices.

Slow-Cooked Pumpkin and Sage Risotto

Ingredients

- 1 cup Arborio rice
- 2 cups vegetable broth
- 1 cup pumpkin puree
- 1/2 cup grated Parmesan cheese
- 1 small onion, chopped
- 2 garlic cloves, minced
- 1/2 cup white wine
- 2 tbsp butter
- 1 tbsp fresh sage, chopped
- Salt and pepper to taste

Instructions

1. In a slow cooker, combine the Arborio rice, vegetable broth, pumpkin puree, Parmesan, onion, garlic, and white wine.
2. Stir to mix well.
3. Cover and cook on low for 3-4 hours, stirring occasionally, until the rice is tender and the risotto is creamy.
4. Stir in butter, fresh sage, salt, and pepper before serving.

Slow-Cooked Beef and Barley Soup

Ingredients

- 1 lb beef stew meat, cut into cubes
- 1 cup pearl barley
- 4 cups beef broth
- 2 carrots, chopped
- 2 celery stalks, chopped
- 1 onion, chopped
- 2 garlic cloves, minced
- 1 tsp dried thyme
- 1 tsp dried rosemary
- Salt and pepper to taste
- Fresh parsley for garnish

Instructions

1. In a slow cooker, combine the beef stew meat, barley, beef broth, carrots, celery, onion, garlic, thyme, rosemary, salt, and pepper.
2. Cover and cook on low for 7-8 hours, until the beef is tender and the barley is cooked through.
3. Garnish with fresh parsley before serving.